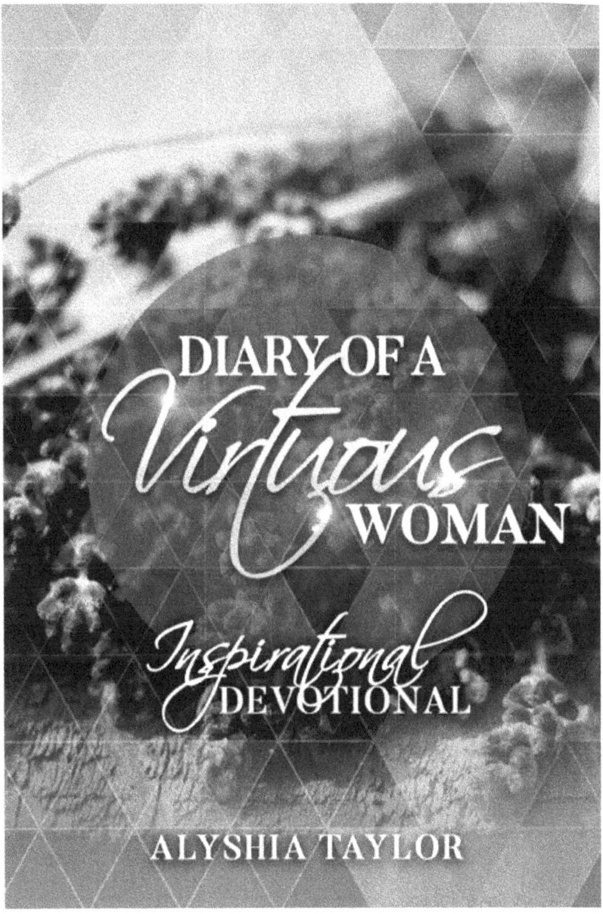

Diary of A Virtuous Woman
Inspirational Devotional

by
Alyshia Taylor

Copyright © [2017] by [Alyshia Taylor]
www.AlyshiaTaylor.com

All rights reserved. No part of this book may be reproduced, scanned,
or distributed in any printed or electronic form without permission.
First Edition: April 2017
Printed in the United States of America
ISBN: 978-0692865101

Published by Vision Directives
www.VisionDirectives.com

Cover Design by Minor Design Co.

VISION|DIRECTIVES

To My Husband and Daughter,
You Mean The World To Me

Acknowledgement

I'd like to acknowledge, God's Miracle Ministry for Deliverance Inc., Impact Deliverance Ministry, Vision Directives, My Mother, Breonna Hairston, Josephine Smith, Pastor Jacqueline Bynum, Elder Bobby Bynum, Associate Pastor William Andrew Taylor, Donnell Grace, Wesley Hairston Sr., Adrienne Hairston, Shanita Swann, Erica Eshun, Sada Boyd, Destinee McCrea, Elder Lisa Milliner Keen, Ashley Richardson, Tavin Littlejohn, Kia Diggs, Valencia Cannon, Renee Cooper, Janelle Middleton, Sr. Pastor Steven Shaw, Pastor Darlene Shaw..

Dear Reader,

Thank you for the interest in purchasing this book. I have written this book in hopes of helping others who may have dealt with similar issues that you will soon read.

After reading this book you will feel confident, motivated, encouraged, & inspired; most importantly a desire to draw closer to the Lord and make the best decision for the next step in your life.

I hope that you enjoy this book. You are beautiful, you are strong, and you are victorious. God bless you.

Alyshia R. Taylor

Dear Diary,

Today is the day of a new beginning. Sigh… I need to get it to together because I have a beautiful baby girl and a handsome husband. Life is entirely too short to be feeling like this. I think I need some help. This is not me, my strength is weak, my thoughts and feelings are all over the place. I have to get back on point. Well it's time to put this pencil down, time to get ready for work. I will finish writing tomorrow.

Sometimes in life you will feel like there is nothing more to it, but you have to get up and keep going

Alyshia Taylor

Dear Diary,

Last night I got some good rest. It was sooo good that I feel like going back to sleep. I believe that I will be ok, later today I'll be going to see someone to talk about how I have been feeling. Before I go I am going to fix me and baby girl breakfast and have a good time it will keep my mind off some things that I know I shouldn't be thinking about. Tomorrow is Saturday so after this appointment trying to plan a fun weekend ought to be nice. There will be great news to write about Monday.

When making a decision about yourself, make sure that your mind is clear and that you are focusing on positivity

Dear Diary,

The weekend was alright. Today I feel like a happy person, just happy with life, my daughter, and my job. When it comes to my marriage though being happy is not the best term to describe for that. Friday my visit to the clinic downtown on Main St. was weird all what was needed was an ID to answer a few questions, talked to someone about thirty minutes, they gave me a brochure about feelings and sent me on my way. Not the help that was expected. Getting ready to cook dinner so I can feed my lil' mama and watch TV. Today is Monday oh yea I got to go my show criminal minds come on tonight can't miss that.

*Happiness starts within,
once you feel that happiness inside, it can become contagious*

Alyshia Taylor

Dear Diary,

Whew!! My husband woke me up this morning about 5:00am all I can hear was him getting ready for work. I wanted to scream CAN YOU BE QUIET!!! Instead I just turned over in the bed to try to go back to sleep. I couldn't so I went ahead and got up as I sat on the side of the bed I began to ponder about our marriage. He works 12 hours a day, 6 days a week. I work maybe four or five days, 8 hours a day. The days that I have off I spend with my baby, and when he has days off he rests which is well understood but when we have days off together I never knew we were off on the same day until the next week. We don't sleep in the bed together, we don't eat together, and we spend no time together starting to feel like roommates, Wow!!! Come to think about it we have not even been intimate in a while. Hmmm

Don't allow your feelings to rob you of sleep, you are able to focus better when you are fully energized

Dear Diary,

For the last past few days I have been thinking about when my husband woke me up when he was getting ready for work that day. So today I will try to talk to him, we have been married for almost two-years now and for a year in a half I have not been happy. Maybe actually talking about it will help. Every time I try to talk to him he never feels like talking. Oh I forgot to mention that I registered for the community college today. I take a placement test next week I am interested in the nursing program I love helping people.

> *Once you notice that your happiness has died, address the issue before it gets too late or it will become harder to deal with*

Dear Diary,

I'm back again, I didn't get a chance to talk to my husband yesterday but it's cool. I feel like I will never understand what's going on between us. Before we said our vows to each other we did things together all the time. We talked to each other more but for the past year it just seems like he's not interested in this marriage or me. Did I mention that he was a different religion?? I am trying to think if maybe that had anything to do with the change. It shouldn't we both knew what we were getting ourselves into before we agreed to spend the rest of our lives together. Wow!!

Overthinking can lead to misinterpretation, don't keep yourself guessing it will always lead to confusion

Dear Diary,

Yesterday I made an appointment with a different facility to really be able to talk to someone, I am starting to believe that the way I have been feeling has a lot to do with what I am dealing with emotionally. I have a husband that does not talk to me, he does not even tell me how pretty I am, we don't go out, he makes me feel like I am not beautiful, when we do talk on the phone I tell him that I love him and his response back is ok, like what happened to the words I love you too?? When he comes home from work he takes a shower, and then he leaves I never know where he is going and when I do ask the response he gives me is "I am going out" I see how he talks to other people he is so happy, giggly, and bubbly but when I attempt to talk to him I get a different reaction, I get ignored.

Sigh, this hurts.

*I didn't love myself, had I loved myself,
his actions would not have been able to control me
emotionally*

Alyshia Taylor

Dear Diary,

What am I doing wrong? I work, I cook every single day, I clean, I do laundry, I iron clothes, I make sure that baby girl is well taken care of and whenever my husband feels like having sex I have it with him. Even though we don't have sex often when we do I don't enjoy it. I can't even turn him on. Did he marry me because he had a different agenda? I do all that a wife is supposed to do, plus more and I still get treated like a nobody. I am not only now emotionally disturbed; I am now mentally disturbed. I can't spend the rest of my life like this feeling unwanted and miserable. All my friends are happy with their marriage & I want to be happy just like them. I would love to take trips and vacations, and enjoy life but he has no interest in that kind of stuff, I don't see why not we make enough money to cover all of the expenses for a trip; but hey, wishful thinking.

I know that I am a good person, I will continue to remain that good person even if I am not acknowledged for it, one day it will take me far

Alyshia Taylor

Dear Diary,

Today was an okay day, But I thank God that I am alive I can't complain. I went to take my placement test today at the college; I didn't do so well I could not focus with so much going on at home. Bre and I had some fun today. She started walking. When it's only just me and Bre I feel so happy, and then when I get around my husband I get so angry. I like to be happy all the time, especially since I have a family at home. My husband is supposed to be my best friend, but instead he feels like an enemy. Everything that comes out of his mouth is something that's hurtful, never anything encouraging or positive. I can barely get a hello or how was your day, I am afraid that I cannot last in this marriage much longer. Time for bed now, it's getting late.

When your days don't go as planned & your thoughts begin to take over, find Joy in something that has happened, only if it was just waking up to another day

Dear Diary,

Last night I didn't go straight to sleep I cried my eyes out, I feel lost, but confident. I have made a final decision to pack me and baby girl things up and leave. I am not sure as to where I will be taking us, but I am getting out of here. Every involvement I have ever had with a man I always get hurt. I never imagined that being married would cause more emotional and mental stress. This is the worst relationship that I have ever been in. I hate me for this, what was I thinking? I do love Amos, but being in love I am realizing I never was. I feel like I wasted a year and a half of my life. How could I not see that I am with someone who does not love me? I will keep trusting God and believing that he will work it all out for me.

Weeping may endure for a night, but joy cometh in the morning. Psalms 30:5

Dear Diary,

Today is my dad's birthday. He passed away a few months ago I wish he were here to talk to. When Amos came home this evening he realized that I have some things packed up. Of course now he wants to talk. I literally don't have anything to say, I will give it a try though. He asked why was I packing and where was I going. This was the perfect opportunity to attempt to express how I have been feeling, and my thoughts. Before I began to speak he shuts me off by saying that he loves me and that he does not want me to go, he says himself how he knows that he has not been treating me the best, he's kissing on me and pulling my clothes off, he begins to nibble on my breast and lick my neck, I can see the stiffness of his penis arising through his pants, before I knew it he is on top of me, I am not in the mood for this but I just shut my mouth and laid there. As we are having sex all I can think of

was how emotionally destroyed I have become and how my feelings are numb towards him. The more he strokes the harder he does it and he's whispering in my ear that I am not going to leave. He's smacking me in the face asking me where I am going. He won't let me up after I asked him to stop; he squeezes my neck until I feel like I can no longer breath. Feels like a monster on the top of me. The only thing that loosened the tightness of the grip of his hand around my neck is that he ejaculated and pulls out of me. He then he yells FINE!!! Go wherever you want to go, it's up to you. If he really loved me like he said, then why would he treat me like this or tell me to just go?

*Ye though I walk through the valley of the shadow of death,
I will fear no evil, thy rod & thy staff they comfort me. Psalms 23*

Dear Diary,

Happy 4th of July! It's hard for me to gain focus after last night episode. I have never seen Amos act like this. I have a light bruise around my neck, and a little mark on my face, the plan today was to go downtown and enjoy the festivities and have fun. There is no way to cover up my face or my neck, it's impossible for me to step out and go anywhere. I am afraid that I will run into someone that I know, even worse people will be looking at me. It will just be to embarrassing. I know now that I have to go searching for a place to stay and first thing in the morning, I will be making some phone calls.

* When you are overwhelmed with racing thoughts take a deep breath, pray, and allow God to take over.

Alyshia Taylor

Dear Diary,

Yesterday I made some phone calls around at some shelters, most of them said that I would have to fill out an application. After I explained to them that I have experienced some violence I was told that I needed a police report. I don't want to go to the police I just want to get out of this house and away from him. I also applied to some low-income houses today, the manager I spoke with told me that I will go on a waiting list and that they will give me a call or send a letter once my name became closer on the top of the list for assistance it will take at least 6 months he said. Until then I will apply at more places, save my money, keep some of my things packed until that day comes to be able to move.

* Those that wait upon the Lord shall renew their strength,
& mount up with wings like an eagle, they shall run & not weary, walk & not faint. Isaiah 40:31

Dear Diary,

This was my weekend to work, and boy was it busy. Yes, indeed it was. It's good I worked the weekend it kept my mind off a lot, my co-workers asked me what happened & I can hear them whispering "Girl do you see her" the customers were looking at me like they saw a ghost, even though it was hard to do I still gave them a smile though.

Last night when Amos got home he looked at me and laughed; he asked me "do you actually think that you are going to leave?" I did not respond back I tried to ignore him and watch TV. He repeated the same question this time even louder with an aggressive tone. I still ignored him, seconds later I feel a punch in my arm. I begged him not tonight please....

Then punches continued they went from my arm to my face. I tried my best to defend myself, I want to call the police but I am afraid, maybe the reason why he's acting like this is because he loves me and he wants me to stay. If I didn't ignore him he probably would have not hit me, next time I will just to answer him.

* For God hath not given us the spirit of fear but of power, and of love, and of a sound mind. 2 Timothy 1:7

Dear Diary,

Was supposed to work today but I called out. I feel like quitting my job altogether and running away. What am I here for? I am not a punching bag to anybody. Everyday it has been something. I hate coming home, the only reason that I do come is so that baby girl can have a place to eat and sleep. I just know pretty soon all this will change, God please help me get out of this. Please God, Please!!!!!!!!!

* God is our refuge and strength, a very present help in trouble.
Psalms 46:1

Dear Diary,

It's Friday the 13th I am not one to believe in bad luck and all that stuff, I have been through hell all week. I am going to start back reading my bible and taking notes of what I read to keep my everyday life going. I plan to pick up a second job so I can save some money for Christmas for baby girl, and so we can leave. I just know real soon that something is going to change for me. I still love my husband after all he is doing to me, but I AM NOT IN LOVE with him. I need to get my life back, I have not been to church in a while and God comes first. I am waiting on the Lord to speak to me, I feel like I made a big mistake. What I thought Amos could do for me, God can do even more; I started depending on a man instead of God, Shame on me.

* Better to trust in the Lord than to put confidence in princes. Psalms 118:8

Dear Diary,

Today was the first day I picked my bible back up and read it. I researched some scriptures about marriage, one I read was (2 Corinthians 6:14-18) I began to read about how God said in his word to not be unequally yoked with non-believers, and he will then receive me and become a father to me after I separate myself from it and not touch the unclean thing. I also read something in the book of (Ephesians 5:25) about how the husband are to love their wives as Christ love the church and gave his life for her. This fool don't know nothing about Christ because he practices something else, but I do though. Yea, it's time to get myself together.

*I got so caught up into me that I fell off. Do not to lose yourself while trying to find someone else.

Dear Diary,

Yesterday when I read, and what I read, motivated me to keep going and to get back to God. Today I read in the book of (Romans 8:38-39) it said to not let anything separate us from the love of Christ. I am going to take it step by step, day by day, the beatings still occur and after the beatings he wants sex, then after sex he wants me to cook if I do not cook before he gets back then comes an argument. But I just stay quiet, and go along with the flow, I will pray and keep reading the word and build my faith back to God. I feel like God is disappointed in me. Maybe everything that I am going through is because I put myself in something that I had no knowledge of, maybe if I knew then my antenna would of went off or red flags would of went up for me to know. I'm learning as I go though.

* He giveth power to the faint; and to them that have no might he increaseth strength.
Isaiah 40:29

Dear Diary,

Checked the mail today, a letter came from the low-income housing it said Dear Ms. Alyshia, we have reviewed your application and would like for you to call our office to set up an appointment for further process to see if you are approved. This letter came so fast, the manager told me a waiting list of six months and here it is less than the time he told me, this is definitely a sign that it's time to go, I ran upstairs and hidden the letter in one of my drawers so that Amos would not see it. (Matthew 6:33) it said to seek the kingdom of God first and his righteousness and all things shall be added unto you. God I thank you.

> * Trust in the Lord with all thine heart; and lean not unto thine own understanding.
> Proverbs 3:5

Dear Diary,

Worked a long shift today, my feet are hurrrrting. Last past few days Amos has not said a word, not complaining, the peace is needed right now. There is an opportunity to do some overtime at work of course I signed up for a few weeks that way when it's time to move there will be enough money saved to do what it is that needs to be done so I will be able to proceed and press forward. I am off this weekend and guess who is going to church? Yep, this girl. For once I feel like everything is going really good.

* When you are waiting on the Lord be patient, be positive, & have faith.

Dear Diary,

Church today was exactly what I needed; the Pastor preached a good word. I went down to rededicate my life back to the Lord, and also for prayer one of the ministers that prayed for me told me that God said to trust him more. That I will be doing, I just feel at ease. The inside of me still feels discouraged, but mentally I feel free. When I got home I went to the mirror and said to myself enough is enough, reading (Proverbs 18:21) I learned that death and life are in the power of the tongue. So before I cooked I started saying things like; I will survive, I will not die, I will be happy, I will keep going and I will trust you God I began to feel encouraged. Amos walked in and heard me told me I needed to shut up. I kept talking, I paid him no attention he hit me in my mouth and yelled: didn't I say shut up. I can taste the blood; even though I shut my lips I still said these things in my head.

* Turn, O backsliding children, saith the Lord; for I am married unto you.
I will take you one of a city, and two of a family and I will bring you to Zion. Jeremiah 3:14

Dear Diary,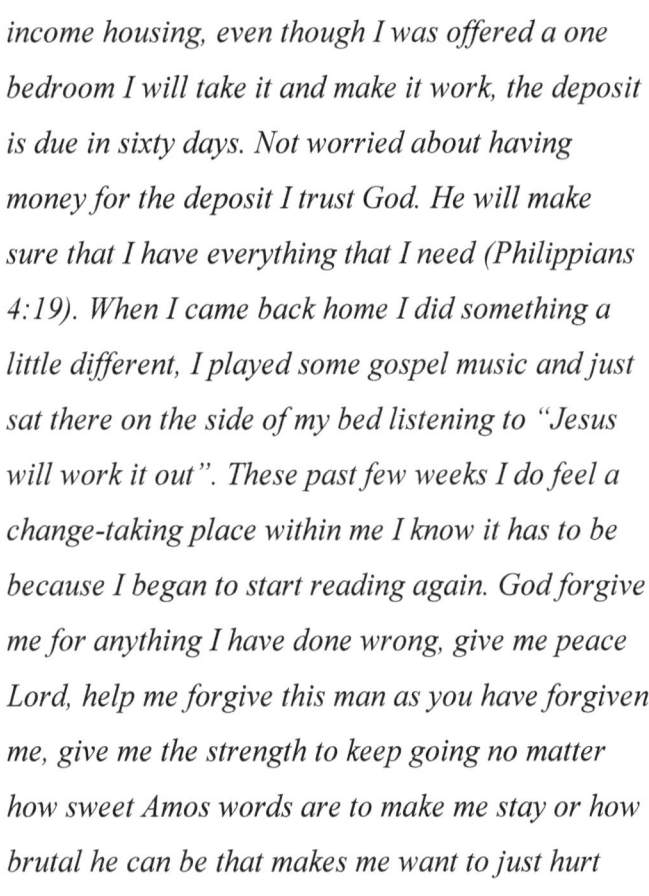

I was approved for the low income housing, even though I was offered a one bedroom I will take it and make it work, the deposit is due in sixty days. Not worried about having money for the deposit I trust God. He will make sure that I have everything that I need (Philippians 4:19). When I came back home I did something a little different, I played some gospel music and just sat there on the side of my bed listening to "Jesus will work it out". These past few weeks I do feel a change-taking place within me I know it has to be because I began to start reading again. God forgive me for anything I have done wrong, give me peace Lord, help me forgive this man as you have forgiven me, give me the strength to keep going no matter how sweet Amos words are to make me stay or how brutal he can be that makes me want to just hurt him. Lord I need you.

*Commit thy ways unto the Lord; trust also in him; and he shall bring it to pass. Psalms 37:5

Dear Diary,

Truck day at the job, that's some good news I can get the boxes to save for packing some more. I'm on my lunch break just thinking how proud I am of myself and reminiscing when Amos and me first met compared to how he treats me now. I miss the days where I was treated good, but I don't miss them so bad that I want to stay. At this point I need to focus. The little friends I do have they ain't got time to hear my problems. I have to be careful whom I talk to anyway, writing my thoughts seem better. Well my break is almost over, I hear somebody calling my name. I will write again soon.

* Talk to God more & friends less. He will direct & lead your path.

A Virtuous Woman

Dear Diary,

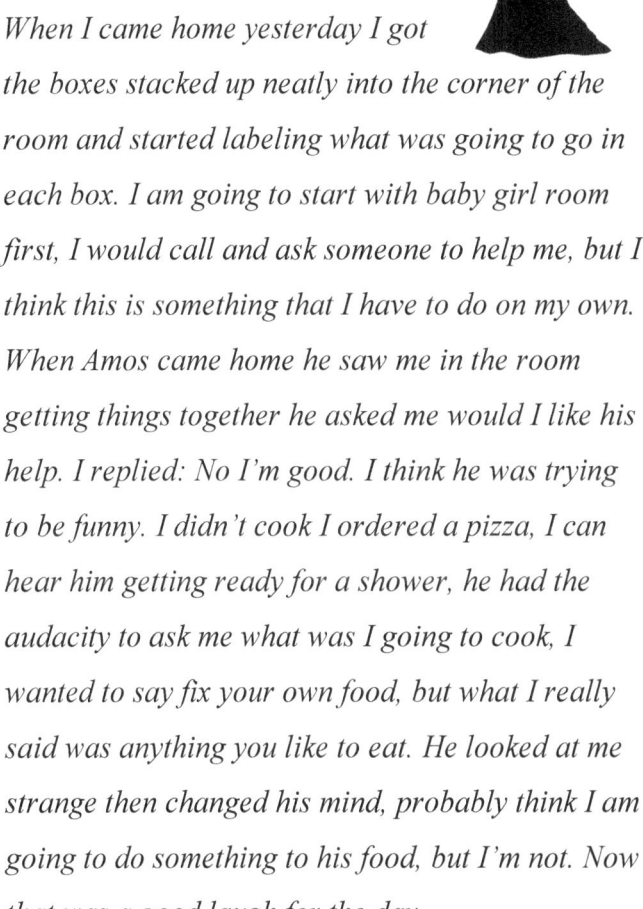

When I came home yesterday I got the boxes stacked up neatly into the corner of the room and started labeling what was going to go in each box. I am going to start with baby girl room first, I would call and ask someone to help me, but I think this is something that I have to do on my own. When Amos came home he saw me in the room getting things together he asked me would I like his help. I replied: No I'm good. I think he was trying to be funny. I didn't cook I ordered a pizza, I can hear him getting ready for a shower, he had the audacity to ask me what was I going to cook, I wanted to say fix your own food, but what I really said was anything you like to eat. He looked at me strange then changed his mind, probably think I am going to do something to his food, but I'm not. Now that was a good laugh for the day.

* Be a woman of integrity, don't miss out on your blessing because of the actions of others.

Dear Diary,

I woke up in the middle of the night from a dream of me putting a flame to Amos, as he was asleep on the couch, it felt so real. Maybe the dream came from all the times that I never did anything to retaliate against him, it truly is hard looking at someone in the face daily who you really have no desire for I guess I can understand how he feels about me. Even though I'm moving forward it's hard because I still hurt on the inside, this is not easy. Sometimes I want him to hurt just like I hurt then I ask myself what is that going to solve? Evil for evil is not good; you are supposed to overcome evil with good. (Romans 12:21)

> *Bless those that curse you, and pray for them, which despitefully use you.
> Luke 6:28

Dear Diary,

Whew!! Tired, tired, tired every day when I get home from work I pack a lil bit here, a lil bit there stop take a rest and get back at it. Today when Amos came home he decides to tell me that the Television will be staying with him, the couches, the pictures, and the dishes. Okay!! I don't care he can keep all of that stuff at least the moving truck won't have to be so big I can make one trip. He thinks he hurting me but whatever. He got in my face asking who you going to find to pay the bills, who you going to find to help you, I replied: I found God!! Oh his mouth ain't say nothing else after that. Sometimes you have to shut the devil up. Going to finish packing I will be back soon.

> * And I will restore unto you the years that the locust hath eaten, the cankerworm, and the caterpillar, and the palmerworm, my great army

which I sent among you. And ye shall eat in plenty and be satisfied, and praise the name of the Lord your God that hath dealt wondrously with you: and my people shall never be ashamed. Joel 2:25-26

Dear Diary,

Tonight is Bible Study I will try my best to get there, I decided to go through some papers and I found that Amos has been sending money to someone, I'm not talking about forty or fifty dollars I am talking about three or four hundred dollars & all he gives me is forty dollars every paycheck to help me Tuh! Now I see why. This man has a whole separate bank account with another bank,

I have found pornos, and brand condoms that we don't use. What kind of married man keeps this kind of stuff? I even found out that he has planned a vacation but it's all fine & dandy.

See when God is getting ready to do something in your life or you are about to be blessed the enemy has a way of trying to get in the way. I do admit that I am surprised but there is bigger fish I have to fry and my life I have to live. I refuse to give up now.

*And this I speak for your own profit; not that I may cast a snare upon you, but for that which is comely, and that ye may attend upon the Lord without distraction. 1 Corinthians 7:35

Dear Diary,

Yesterday was a busy day, if it has not been one thing it's another I was just informed at the last minute that Amos will be going overseas for a month, I think he knew, he just ain't want to tell me, he leaves in two days, am I mad? No, but I plan to be completely gone before he gets back, he will not be able to find me, I plan to use this month that he is gone to start restoring with no distractions, I don't have to worry about him coming home taking my joy. Everything I found the other day I want to know what is going on but if I was to bring it up I know for a fact that it will be an argument so letting peace be still is the best thing to do right now.

When the enemy shall come in like a flood,
the Spirit of the Lord shall lift up a standard against him.
Isaiah 59:19

Dear Diary,

Amos left early this morning, did not even say a word like good-bye, but look who I'm talking about here. This evening an eviction notice was stuck in the door the rent has not been paid for July, a phone call that if there is no payment by 5pm today the lights will be off tomorrow, and then another letter stating that the water will be disconnected in the morning. Even though our marriage is basically done how can he leave the country knowing that he did not pay a dime for anything this month. He left us with nothing. Not even a piece of bread. God has plan. I Trust God.
(Proverbs 3:5-6)

> * Trusting God can be very hard, but you must continue to walk by faith& not by sight.

Dear Diary,

Ahhhh!!!! I had to get that out, yesterday was one of those days. Even though all these obstacles are in the way, VICTORY IS MINES!!! The money that was saved up for me to move I used to catch up all the bills. Do I feel discouraged? No, Do I feel motivated? Yes!!! There is no way that I was going to let my child be sitting in the dark, with no food or water, nor not have a place to stay. No one knows the things that I am going through, it's hard to tell or even trust someone without them looking down on you. At this point it really is just me and God! I was so close to being on the way out the door I feel like I am stuck here, it's like he set me up. Gas tank is on E, fridge is a little light, and my account says negative $125 when my check gets deposited there still won't be much. My faith right now is stronger than ever my trust is fully in the Lord & this is what I'm going to do. I will look to the hills *from whence my help cometh from, my help cometh from the Lord (Psalms 121).*

* God has a way of always making a way out of no way. You will never go without.

Dear Diary,

On the way to work I got a phone call from an unknown number, come to find out that It was Amos. He left a voicemail telling me that he didn't pay anything towards bills that he hopes that I can find a way to pay them. I laughed & deleted the message that was not going to ruin my day. I have made up in my mind that I will keep it stayed on Jesus, he will keep me in perfect peace (Isaiah 26:3). I declare and decree that no matter what I will keep pressing my way through. I am a very strong woman to stay here & put up with the mess Amos does, but I am an even stronger woman because I have Jesus. I know that no man can do any harm to me because I have Jesus. I'm finding myself. And I notice that the more I have leaned towards the Lord, he is leaning towards me. Amos will not be able to make me feel like I'm a no body anymore I know who I am. I AM A WOMAN OF

GOD!!

* I allowed being married make me blind to who I am, a man should be able to push you closer to God rather than pull you away.

A Virtuous Woman

Dear Diary,

Left church today & did not feel the same way I felt when I went in, the decision I made to finally leave my husband and turn to God was the best decision ever. Tuesday I will take out a loan to be able to move. Everything is absolutely going to work out. All things work together to those who are called, and love the lord. (Romans 8:28) I believe God's word. Maybe Amos being gone is going to be good for right now, a few days ago I felt like I was not going to be able to proceed. The devil is liar.

* Believe in yourself when nobody else does, many of your greatest accomplishments start with you.

Dear Diary,

Guess what?? I was approved for a loan; they approved me for more than I needed. I went ahead and called the moving truck company to reserve a truck, and then I got a money order to pay the deposit on the apartment. After I pay the utilities & first month rent I will get my keys. I was able to stop by the grocery store and shop some. I thought that I was down to nothing. Boom! Here comes more than what I had the first time. I know that it had been because of faith. When I got home today there was a knock at the door, one of Amos' friends said he stopped by to check on us because he knows that Amos does not treat me right. Before he left he handed me this white envelope. I opened it and inside there was money with a note that said, "Use this to pay your bills, and don't worry about paying it back." I could have shouted all night long. I'm about to get ready for bed. Tonight will be a peaceful sleep.

　* All you need is faith the size of a mustard seed and you will be able to move mountains.

Alyshia Taylor

Dear Diary,

Everything is all packed up; I can't explain how this feels. I can't explain how it feels to come home every day & not be mad, I can't explain how it feels coming home and worshipping and praising God and I don't have to be quiet, I can't explain how it feels to come home and for once not argue & cry. I can't explain how it feels to come home & not get beat because I just want to stay to myself, I can't explain how it feels to no longer have to pretend to be happy when I'm not. So far this has been the best two weeks I have had in a long time. I'm able to think freely and meditate. I'm very thankful and I owe everything to God, if it had not been for God by my side & on my side I don't know where I would be.

*Even when we were dead in sin, hath quickened us
together with Christ,
by Grace ye are saved.
Ephesians 2:5

A Virtuous Woman

Dear Diary,

This weekend has been AMAZIIIING!!!! All I keep hearing in my ear is freedom, freedom, freedom. Amos made me feel like I could not make it without him, and I actually believed that I probably couldn't. He called again today I mean he blew my phone UP! If I answered I know that there would have been a possibility that he might say something that would aggravate me, I ain't got time for it, even though in the back of my mind I wonder what it is that he wants. Okay I gave in Lol! I answered by the time I said hello the phone hung up now that was my cue that I didn't need to talk to him Lol! It's 10:30 p.m. time to take my behind to bed.

* So then faith comes by hearing, and hearing by the word of God.
Romans 10:17

Dear Diary,

I got all the way to work today only to find out that I had the day off, I guess I read the schedule wrong. I promise that somebody changed it. But it's all cool though instead of coming back home I rode to the lake, parked my car in a shady area, laid back and turned on some music. As the tears poured out of my eyes and down to my face all I could do was thank God for what he is bringing me out of. Nobody will ever convince me that God is not real. My prayers are being answered, that's a for sure sign that God hears me. In a few weeks I will officially be in a new place, a place that I can say that is my own.

> * I have gained confidence, and God gets all the glory he makes all things new.

Dear Diary,

Today was the day of the appointment that I scheduled a few months ago. Things have been going so well I have forgotten all about it. I filled out a questionnaire waited a bit then I was called back into some room. Moments later someone came in I was sweating like a pig I was so nervous. The person introduced herself as one of the doctors, so anyway we started talking. Throughout our conversations I express the internal feeling of what I had been coping with in comparison as to how I feel now. By the end of our session she seemed so amused, because we ran out of time I was scheduled to come back. I can't wait to go back it felt good to finally talk to someone.

*Conversing with a person who can relate with you can be a great thing.
Allow yourself to share what you want to be shared.

Dear Diary,

I have been extremely busy and exhausted that I have not had a chance to sit and write. The good news is that I have moved into my place. Everything is all settled in the only thing I have to do is make a trip to the grocery store so I can cook our first meal. I have a welcome doormat at the front door,

I have pictures of Bre & me on the walls, a set of cream-colored curtains hung up to the windows that match the carpet in the living room. My bathroom is decorated in purple & pink, my kitchen is decorated in red, and my bedroom is set up for a queen & princess. This feels good. If I had not stepped out on faith, and not put my trust in the Lord I believe that I still would be living in misery.

Finally called my family up told them that I had move. Their reaction was clueless; they'll be by later today to check me out. Gotta go get ready for work I got these bills to pay.

I like the way that sounds. "I" got these bills to pay. Lol! I'm proud of myself.

   * But he that glorieth, let him glory in the Lord.
                2 Corinthians 10:17

Dear Diary,

The change that I always talked about that I knew was going to happen is finally here. My next step is to file for legal separation papers. Divorce is something that I don't believe in doing, but I have to do what I got to do in order to move on with my life. I have no regrets that I married Amos, in fact I appreciate it all. I realize that if it had not been for the nights sleeping alone, the times my husband did not talk to me, the days I would get beat and still have to maintain household duties, go to work, and be a mother. All the words that were spoken to break me, the hurt, the shame, the times I cried aloud and the times I cried inside, the depression, the bondage, the mental stress, the emotional stress, there were days that I did not eat because I could not eat, smile when I did not want to smile. I had to go through this to get back to God who is my first love (Revelation 2:4) a man that I will never leave again. I would have never known how strong, wise, victorious, ambitious, beautiful, trustworthy, honest, dependable, I was. Everything that was taken from me I am getting it all back. (Joel 2:25) This Joy I have the world didn't give it & the world cannot take it away. I have a smile now that can brighten up the entire room, I have a light down on the inside that will never go dim again but will shine even brighter through obstacles and situations, the words I speak are full of wisdom & kindness, not doubt or fear, I have a prayer that can reach the heavens, I walk in authority, I walk with power, I wake up fearing the Lord, & my daily desire is to serve him. I understand my worth, I have a vision, I have a goal & God has the plan. I know that I'm above and not beneath, I know that I'm blessed & highly favored, I know that everything that I touch will prosper & not fail, I'm Proverbs 31. I am a VIRTUOUS WOMAN!!!

* He that overcometh shall inherit all things; and I will be his God and he shall be my son.
Revelation 21:7

Alyshia Taylor

ABOUT THE AUTHOR

Alyshia is a native of Greensboro, North Carolina; she attended Bennett Middle College, an all-girl high school, and graduated in 2004. Writing since the age of eight years old, she started out writing poems and then the poems turned into the hobby of daily writing. Alyshia was inspired to write as a way of expressing her personal thoughts and feelings. Alyshia is a devoted wife, mother, & friend who loves the Lord and believes in putting him first. She is also an ordained Minister of the Gospel of Jesus Christ under the Leadership of Pastor Jacqueline & Elder Bobby Bynum of God's Miracle Ministry for Deliverance Inc. in her hometown of Greensboro, North Carolina. Along with her many accomplishments, Alyshia has a degree in cosmetology and early childhood education. She is a woman of faith, integrity, respect, and purpose with a personality that is one of a kind.

www.ingramcontent.com/pod-product-compliance
Lightning Source LLC
Chambersburg PA
CBHW070106100426
42743CB00012B/2664